I0119561

Simon M. Landis

Prison-Life Thoughts

Practical, Sharp, Eccentric and Humorous

Simon M. Landis

Prison-Life Thoughts
Practical, Sharp, Eccentric and Humorous

ISBN/EAN: 9783744762434

Printed in Europe, USA, Canada, Australia, Japan

Cover: Foto ©Suzi / pixelio.de

More available books at **www.hansebooks.com**

PRACTICAL, SHARP, ECCENTRIC AND HUMOROUS.

PRISON-LIFE THOUGHTS!

BY

SIMON M. LANDIS, M.D., D.D.,

THE PROGRESSIVE CHRISTIAN.

Written during his confinement in the Philadelphia County Prison
for Publishing his Great Scientific Physiological Book,

ENTITLED

"THE SECRETS OF GENERATION."

☞ Editors are welcome to quote these "Thoughts"
by crediting them to Dr. Landis.

PUBLISHED BY
"LANDIS PUBLISHING SOCIETY."
PHILADELPHIA, PA.
1872.

Entered according to Act of Congress, in the year 1872, by

SIMON M. LANDIS, M.D., D.D.,

In the Office of the Librarian of Congress, at Washington, D. C.

PREFACE.

Dr. S. M. LANDIS, the founder of the PROGRESSIVE CHRISTIAN CHURCH of Philadelphia, was arrested, given a mock trial, and imprisoned by the Pharisees for his Religious Innovations, as will be seen by carefully perusing his "*Prison-Life Thoughts.*"

Landis says that the "Church of God," as established by Christ, consists of all the "wonderful works" and fixed laws of the Creator—all of which have been created for man's Generation and Regeneration. Therefore, to become scientific, *bonâ fide*, practical, live Christians, we must learn and live out the infallible laws of Generation and Regen-

eration; thus, we have the key to the kingdom of heaven, and by becoming practical
observers of the laws of Generation, and laws
of " Healing," or Growing, or Regeneration,
we shall improve the human race, who will
thereby re-inherit sound bodies and sound
minds or souls; causing man to again become
the "Temple of God," undefiled; when the
" Image of God," or image of perfection, will
be enthroned, and man will hold pre-eminence
over the brute creation, giving him dominion
over every beast, and over the brutal desires
of a degenerate humanity; when the Spirit
of God will intuitively manifest itself to all
rational creatures, and His will be done here
in earth as it is there in heaven !

"*Prison-Life Thoughts* " were written during Landis' solitary confinement in Moya-
mensing Prison, at Philadelphia, Pa.   He

entered the Prison Jan. 22, 1870, and was pardoned and exonerated by Governor JOHN W. GEARY, May 19, 1870, making his confinement four months all but four days.

From the Philadelphia Evening Bulletin.

(FROM HARRISBURG, PA.)

THE PARDON OF DR. LANDIS.

HARRISBURG, *May* 19. The following is the substance of the pardon just issued to Dr. S. M. Landis, of Philadelphia, sentenced to one year's imprisonment for the publication of obscene books.

"*And whereas :* It has been made known to me by sundry communications, now on file in the office of the Secretary of the Commonwealth, that the book published and sold by the said Simon M. Landis was a medical work, written by himself for the purpose of benefiting the community, and not with the intention, or for the purpose of corrupting or subverting the morals of any one," etc.

1*

The prosecutors and persecutors of Landis, we think, felt as though they were doing God's service to get him out of their way; because he was a thorn in their pious sides for many years, boldly and fearlessly having taught as one having authority. *In fact*, Landis is about one hundred years ahead of the age in which he lives; therefore, neither the prosecutors nor persecutors were capable of comprehending his scientific reformatory movements; hence, they should rather be *pitied*, than *punished* for their ignorance and arrogance!

PRISON-LIFE THOUGHTS.

WHENEVER I want to carry out the Christian mandate: "Love thy neighbor as thyself," some rude gossiper howls out, "Landis is making love to Mrs. Williams." I wish other people would mind their *own* business!

I AM indeed sorry to proclaim it, but it is nevertheless as true as preaching, that the filthiest eaters, drinkers and snifflers claim the most refinement and modesty. They being soiled, require some acts to show that they are not as dirty as they seem; hence, this turning up of noses at natural things.

WHENEVER a person shoves his piety into my face in a business transaction, I always, in such cases, come out better by vehemently clutching my pocket book until he is gone out of sight.

IF wives want to retain the love of their husbands, let them learn to cook and act healthfully, keeping "growed-up," instead of made-up, in bodily charms, when the magnetic attraction will rivet them together as one, indivisible flesh!

NOW-A-DAYS a man is "*made*," (no matter how he lives,) when he has grown old, ugly, and selfish enough to possess more than his share of this world's goods—when his purse is heavier than his brains—and with this *tin* reputation he can wheedle an influence, and command a respectability that must be nauseating to the Almighty himself. It was the power of this metallic conscience that sent me to prison for telling such jolly truths. But, as the Dutchman says, " We are a great peoples ! "

I RATHER think it is an advantage to be in

this prison cell whilst these "*hard times*" last; because, here one is a king, who is clothed, fed, and tutored without bothering about board, tax and rents coming due. I think I will write another book on "Secret" matters when I get out, so I may be re-installed into my old quarters, because "*hard times*" will last as long as blackmailing and political didoes predominate over sound sense and Christianity!

I ALWAYS feel more like praising God when I get close to an innocent, natural, beautiful woman; there seems to be a peculiar something in this part of God's work that transports one to the loftier realms! Dear ladies, I advise you to keep your flesh, nerves, bones and blood clean, by freely using pure air, pure water, pure food, and I assure you, you will not neglect or miss the balance of the real needs and graces which draw one toward you in spite of oneself.

SOLID and fully developed nerves, flesh,

and bones are a trinity in the human race that outweighs all the gold, glitter, and petrifying or pickling panaceas on the continent. Try it on and see.

I NEVER fancied hotel boarding, and, especially *not* this kind, which we guests of the Commonwealth Hot-hell (hotel) get. It is so monotonous-like, and jerked to a fellow, so kind of rudely, through an iron clapper, that it turns the coat of one's stomach, which I hold as being unphysiological.

WHEN the next prayer meeting is held, I wish my persecutors would pray for my release from prison, and *act* upon it, and have me pardoned; if they will do this much for me, I will try my *best* to smoke, chew, and snuff tobacco; eat grease by the pound, and drink strong tea, coffee, wine, and schnapps of all sorts; besides swallow some drugs when sick, and pray God to be delivered from the bad effects of this whole catalogue of defiling poisons; with this *one considera-*

tion, that if my system cannot endure the brunt of this pious revelry, and I flap back into my old habits, that they will not arrest nor imprison me again for this same offence!

IF money-hoarding persons could see themselves as God sees them, they would never want to own more than their share; although they might divide with the poor (who are either too noble and generous-minded or reckless to hold on to *lucre*), and when it came around to their hands again, divide again. Does not God carry on His work in one continual handing around of blessings, upon all alike? Intemperate *lucre* worshippers, please, soberly chew, think, and sleep over this kind of Progressive Christian lore!

YOU may exterminate me, but you cannot kill my sound logic; probably, that is what rouses your ire. If it is, please remember that truth is as valuable to you and yours, as to me and mine; why then make an ape of yourself?

WHEN public officials use their offices to show off their piety and expertness, it is time they were impeached by the people; otherwise, no one knows when he will get his neck into the mouse-trap, and be made sport of, as I was when before an honorable Court, which was surrounded by sots, pimps, moral game-makers (gamblers), and hypocritical cut-throats.

TRUTH when sent up in a skyrocket does not angle around error and pesty insects, but it shoots straight through vice and assimilates with virtue. I am always sorry when any one acknowledges to be shot through by it; because, it is an open confession of sinfulness. Still, it is *no* vice to confess your sins, if by so doing you improve in future hours.

WITH small minds habit makes law; but with God law is that which is infallible. God made laws, and men violate them; but men cannot make laws that God vio-

lates, the chief acts of the pharisee notwithstanding.

LAZINESS breeds worms in living flesh,
and causes the skin to look too dead or too
live.   It is to the flesh of man, what calm
weather is to the stagnant pool of water.

THAT President of a nation, or Governor
of a Commonwealth, who will not pardon
an *innocent* convict, when he knows such
to be the case, is not fit to fill his position ;
or, if he pardons a *guilty* convict for money
or influence, is a contemptible lout.   Such
men should be heroic and competent leaders,
protectors, and instructors to their people,
instead of knucklers and imbeciles !

MORE serious attention is given to breed-
ing good stock of horses, cows, hogs, fish,
dogs, and cats, than to the generation of a
pure-blooded, solid, and sound race of human
beings ; no wonder our Republic is crumb-
ling to pieces ; but, you say it is *not.*   I how-

2

ever *insist* that it is the meanest monarchy on earth,—*filthy lucre* monarchy—everything is sold and bought, from a sucking pig to the highest office of the nation. Fixed law is a fraud.

I HOPE I hate the ways of the Pharisees as much as did Jesus, who pronounced eight most terrible woes upon them. No one can be a decent man, or follower of Christ, who does not despise the ways of these pesty vipers.

SLANG phrases should not be used, except a good can be accomplished by them. A Christian will use anything, even himself in sacrifice, to do good to the many! I have often chained the attention of hardened worldlings by slang language, and by so doing have converted them to truth, nature, and Jesus Christ—fashionable, thin-skinned, modern piety to the contrary notwithstanding.

THERE has been great howling in.this city

(Philadelphia), about the vulgarity and in-
decency of the language I used in my private physiological lectures to the sexes alone,
which I delivered for many years regularly;
but, those who opened their mouths so rudely against me, probably were not any too
pure or wise themselves, or they would not
have been harmed, hurt, nor been canvas-
sing hearsay around grocery and beer shops.
I *alone* knew what was *best* for me to use in
my efforts to instruct the people in God's
fixed laws of human nature.

For example—one evening as my lecture
room was well filled with an intelligent and
refined audience of gentlemen, just before I
commenced to speak, six very rough-looking
fellows—real cut-throats—entered, and the
only empty seats were directly in front of
me. I at once made up my mind that these
men, of the whole crowd, *most* needed sa-
ving; and, therefore, my whole aim was to
get their attention to my remarks, and to do
this, I knew I had to tell some awful vulgar
stories, being aware that good moral audi-

tors would not be harmed by anything I might say, but these cut-throats might be wheedled by giving them assimilable matter interspersed with holy truths., When I rose to speak, three of my men's heads had already bobbed down unto the backs of the seats in front of them, apparently stupefied by the rum in their heads, or asleep. In a clear and jovial manner I began: "Gentlemen, the hour has arrived for the commencement of the lecture, but before entering upon my theme, let me tell you a somewhat VULGAR story." No sooner had I repeated the sentence, "vulgar story," until each of their heads was high up, and their eyes glistened, fully awake to catch every word of smut which was in anticipation. I finished my vulgar story, which was reluctantly given, but it had its good effect, and my men listened to sound logic, which I followed hard-up for some time; however, in about ten minutes I saw a vacillation, a wandering of their thoughts, when I immediately related another *vulgar* and laughable story, and again got full attention; so I continued during the evening. When the lecture was over, I heard one of them say brusquely to the others, "Tom, this is a damn good lecture, we'll come again." "I'll bet you," responded two others. These six men came every week regularly, until I had them weaned from rum, tobacco, gross food, swearing, and they turned out splendid, noble-hearted and whole-souled gentlemen, who have followed me for years, and until I was taken to this cell; and as I was conducted toward the prison, I saw two of them weeping for their *vulgar* lecturer! Now, then, you howling slanderers, where is your wisdom, and my malice and obscenity? Better hide your soft heads under a bushel. I hope a word to the wise will suffice.

MONEY is the God of this universe, and just so long, and in proportion, as you deal honestly with *filthy lucre* (no matter how much you cheat the bodies and souls of men out of their real wants, and spit in God's

2*

face), are you valued by this barbarous, hea-
thenish, degenerate, sectarian, and political
age! Who dare gainsay my Progressive
Christian doctrines?

I DO love sincere and zealously pious
people! There is nothing that can adorn
the human temple, and make it beautiful,
even to the blessed image of God, except
genuine piety; but this kind of piety is not
the same kind that is taught in fashionable
and bigoted sectarian churches,—it is the
piety which causes the disciple to return to
truth, nature, God, and Christ.

IF gossipers, sots, epicures, and usurpers
go to heaven, then I pray to be permitted to
go elsewhere; because they would generate
such smells, sensations, and commotions that
would, to me indeed, be worse than a decent
hell!

OF all contemptible men, he who uses
religion as a cloak to cover up his vices,

is the most dastardly of villains; especially,
if he has been so lucky or favored, as to possess plenty of this world's goods; because,
being rich, could afford to be open and
generous; however, I forgot that riches are
only attained and retained by un-Christ-like
generosity and meanness.

IT is time that the Progressive Christianity, as I have given it to the world in
"*All Sides,*" and "*Sense and Nonsense,*"
should be embraced, as it will guarantee
every member against financial, physical,
and spiritual want. Yea, it will remove
my property and make it *ours; my* God and
make Him *ours; my* interest and make it *ours;*
my business and make it *ours;* in fact, it
will have but one eye single to God's and
man's glory, without selfishness entering
this natural life and Eden gladness! Blackmailing will not be fashionable and respectable then as now, and "*Hard Times*" come
no more.

LOVE is like a dizziness, it makes a person feel so queer that he can't attend to business. That is not original, but the following is:—Love is nothing wrong nor queer, but makes one feel as if he were full of celestial fever, which causes the fine ladies to shiver, still they deem it clever, if the right man comes to offer it ever!

SCIENTIFIC or perfect piety consists in the proper and normal exercise of every inwrought faculty and propensity, so that each one performs its own function; this requires an entirely different culture of the body and mind to what it gets now-a-days.

FREE-LOVE was well defined by my counsel, in the honorable court during my *mock* trial. The moral District Attorney badgered my witnesses, by asking, if "*The First Progressive Christian Church,*" of which I am pastor, was not a free-love church? To which my counsel answered the insolent prosecutor, "If it is a Christian church, it *is* a FREE-LOVE CHURCH. Its members love the truth; love each other and all mankind, even their own personal enemies. They love their neighbors as themselves, and the highest evidence of its being a Christian church would be in their loving *freely* everybody, good, bad or indifferent, wherever man lives throughout God's heritage. Love cannot be too free. Why, gentlemen, love is the strongest word in the Greek language; it is the strongest word in the Anglo-Saxon; it is the strongest word in the English language, come from whatever source it may.

"Love will go beyond the prison or gallows, it will follow the disobedient son to the lowest depths of degradation and vice, it will go with him to the scaffold and beyond the tomb. It will brave a corrupt public sentiment, which to some sensitive souls is more terrible than the gibbet or the rack. GOD IS LOVE, *and he that abideth in God, dwelleth in love, and that continually!*

"The District Attorney did not mean love

at all. He meant if his was not a FREE-LUST church. If you want to find *free-lust,* do not go to a poor, reformatory church, sustained principally by the minister giving nearly all his earnings for that purpose. Such churches have to sacrifice enough from persecution ; being called fanatics, crazy, and their pastors obscene and libellous, without sacrificing themselves to lust. No, rather go to your rich, aristocratic churches, whose ministers travel in Europe at the expense of jealous husbands, if you would find *free-lust.*"

Brother Kilgore, you hit him about in the right place, and no doubt he (and his like) will feel it as long as he lives. I pity and forgive him.

My prison comrades are most lively when I feel disposed to go to sleep at night ; they consist of little mice, big mice; little bugs, bed bugs, and big bugs, sometimes called roaches. They love me better than do the Pharisees, because they dance and make

merry around my head and body, until, in
spite of their entertaining hilarity, I drop to
sleep; this may be esteemed rude, but it is
nevertheless my nature to disregard the conduct of many of God's vermin.

THE day has arrived when an accomoda-
ting Mayor of the great city of Philadelphia
will issue a warrant upon the receipt of a few
letters from pious professors, and arrest a
minister on the Sabbath day in his pulpit,
when he had plenty of time and opportunity
on week days to catch Landis. Something
peeps up that does not exactly look like fit-
ness of office, nor greatness of purpose; but,
then, it gratified the Pharisees, who claim to
own earth, liberty, elements, God, and man!
Great day.

A FRIEND writes me, " Every week you
remain in prison will give you influence
when you get out—you know this, and
ought to be content to be a martyr."
Firstly, How long must an innocent man

remain in a felon's cell to be esteemed a martyr? Secondly, Is there any way by which I can honorably get out of this before my sentence of one year expires? Thirdly, When my year is up, have I enough credit and friends to make me up or loan me the five hundred dollars to pay the fine, which was so generously bestowed upon me for my foolhardiness to attempt to teach the married people how to prevent diseases, unhappiness, and generate sound babies? I am bankrupt in *purse*, but wealthy in *brain*, thank God!

THE only difference between orthodox and progressive Christianity is, that the former saves its members by *"faith,"* no matter what they swallow or breathe; whilst the latter KNOWS that *"faith"* does not change poison to food, nor sinfulness to saintship, but acts DO that chime and harmonize with natural law and godly order; hence, *"good works"* are the foundation of its members, and *"faith"* turns to a perfect trust in the results, without taking drugs or incense!

THE pious old judge who sat on the bench in my trial, at a given point of my counsel's argument, interrupted him and said, " Is this book on the *Secrets of Generation*, a part of Dr. Landis' doctrines of his church?" To which I might here answer his honor, that if his parents had observed the fixed laws that that book taught, their son would have had more sense than to turn the holiest function of maternity into ridicule, and esteem it a good joke for a man who sits in judgment over his fellows.

THERE is a holiness in just indignation which *far* surpasses smooth-tongued hypocrisy.

SOME people think they are very smart and profoundly wise, when (in total ignorance of a *true* Physiology) they assert that *"what you eat has nothing to do with piety or Christianity."* However, it has everything to do with it. First, did not sin come into the world by partaking of poisonous aliment;

3

and, secondly, can a fruit tree bring forth perfect fruit that is not fed upon proper earth and elements? Christianity is the fruit of the tree,—the developed spirit,—which had to depend upon the physical body for its completion! Such people would do well to shut pan and save themselves from exposing their stupidity and ignorance.

ALL the sectarian world says, I am crazy; and *I* say, all the sectarian world is insane or knavish—and they having the majority put me into this prison cell.

IF I could make a slipper out of my keeper, I might quietly pass out of this cell in my stocking feet.

PEOPLE often speak of charitable acts, when they most cruelly cheat human nature of its vitalizing properties; for instance, to be kind to a spoiled child, thereby encouraging him to go on in his wickedness would be cruel, most uncharitable; whereas, to chastise him severely, as good parents do in such cases, would be genuine charity. We hear of too many acts of charity, that are acts of direst cruelty; and many seeming acts of cruelty are *bona fide* acts of charity. There is, after all, nothing like wisdom.

I MAY be esteemed egotistical by saying, that I am confident I have forgotten more practical knowledge than the whole world, at this age, knows; which again confirms my oft repeated assertion, that I esteem all the world insane and they return the compliment, and persecute me for my presumption. Should I pray then for a return to fashionable ignorance and bigotry, and join the Lord-beseeching and dictating crowd, who are either too lazy, blockheaded or rascally to serve Him by "*good works?*"

IT is a pity that thought and meditation cannot be worked into some large machine whereby the settled laws of God could be ground out in tangible bundles, then "seeing

would be believing;" moreover, it would
have saved Christ, and His true followers,
from using the pronouns, I, me, and mine so
much; which is very nauseating to unwise
and ignorant people.

NONE are so foolish as those who claim to
be imperfect, and yet are too bigoted or lazy
to learn even from an enemy.

WHILST modern education makes a person
apt in tricks, customs and civilization, it
nevertheless seems to destroy the natural
intuitive and appreciative power that God
ordained for making man wise, good and
angelic. The more such learning people
generally possess, the more artificial their
tastes, habits and ideas. Birds sing, eat and
breathe without school-training; because,
true to instinct; but, made-up and modern-
ized educated people have no knowledge of
instinct, intuition or holy spirit, unless it be
a hankering for money and lust.

IT is a popular idea that poor men have
no souls; have no right to God's footstool,
because they do not possess sufficient cunning
and meanness to gobble up and hold on to
filthy lucre. Poor fools (?), why should
they be made happy, being too poverty
stricken to be genteel!   The Dutchman
says—Yaw wole! _____

A TRULY great man will always be willing
to sacrifice his own comforts to make his
enemies happy, thus he fulfils the Christian
injunction to "love your enemies."   I feel
complimented by being able to come up to
this stand point of manhood, being assured
that my enemies are so happy at my imprisonment!   I am glad you are delighted,
which makes us both happy!

SOME people delight in the miseries of
others, which deprive themselves of all real
bliss, as there can be no genuine happiness
where a brotherly sympathy, and kindly
aspiration to be good, are lacking.   To be

3*

happy, act to make others likewise, which
will secure *you* the hallowed boon!

MODERN "Popular Sovereignty" bears
upon its daily marred banners—" every man
for himself and the devil catch the hinder-
most;" which Progressive Christianity re-
verses, as follows:—God and all mankind
in unison, and the devil take the selfish
fellow who tries to get ahead of this natural
band of the elect or righteous!

THE narrowest, smallest, meanest mind is
the one who sees the man or woman in the
exterior make-up,—dress and fashionable
fixings,—and neglects to think of the habili-
ments of the inner man or woman!

As God forgives a penitent sinner or
criminal, and Christ came to save or redeem
the repentant, why cannot man take a hint
and do likewise? We reputed criminals
must be locked up in unnatural, filthy cells,
whilst our superiors, who should possess more

of the attributes of God than we, are this
moment chiming their Sabbath bells for holy
worship, whilst we, who most need piety,
can go unexhorted. This looks a little para-
doxical. Wake up, old *vipers*.

I WONDER what verdict and ruling my
honorable Court, (who condescended to notice
me in my prerogatives,) would pronounce
upon natural nudity, were she (the Court)
dropped down into old Eden, where Adam
and ´Eve were naked, and where "wicked
and lewd passions," such as his honor acknowledged *they* possessed, did not exist?
Can any "Public" or private "Ledger,"
inform the prisoner ; which would be no more
difficult, than were the predictions of this
oracle in publishing the " *thanks of the whole
people* " for my incarceration. A man must
truly be great, when the thanks of the *whole
people* are bestowed upon him ! And that
without blackmailing ! I am flattered and
feel jubilant. Try again, SWEET Saints !

—•◦•—

IF the prisoner's " Prison-Life Thoughts"
are *very* brilliant, it must be attributed to
the associations of this civilized Monastery,
and the lessons he has imbibed whilst having
been drilled in the honorable Court of the
Quarter Sessions of Philadelphia, Pennsyl-
vania, U. S. A.   _____

A FEW city Councilmen and ladies called
one day to visit me, one of them, who was
pretty well filled with tobacco, onions and
rum, (if his nose, and the great fumes arising
form his honorable temple are any evidence
of such a conclusion,) entered my cell, and
began to read me a moral lesson on my
impropriety of not having laid by enough
lucre to avert such incarceration; said he:
"A man of your talent ought to have been
smart enough to have made an immense
fortune, by which you could have evaded
this persecution." I was just going to thank
him, when his finely dressed lady came to
the cell-gate, and sarcastically said : "Come,
we must go ; but I guess you think you are

in good hands." To which I had the rudeness to reply : " Madam, the prisoner will not *defile* the Councilman ; please, be not alarmed ! " She hastily left, and he soon followed. Sich is life.

CONVINCE people against their wills, and against their pockets, and you will make the most bitter enemies of the greater proportion of them !

WHEN I hear the Sectarian Church Bells chime on Sundays, whilst in this cell, I feel like plugging up my ears, like Mephistopheles ; knowing that this class are my persecutors, and whilst I am *innocently* confined in a felon's cell, they can go into their brick-and-mortar churches and pray for pardon for their criminal and sinful acts, without ever thinking of turning from error to truth.

A BEAUTIFUL woman or child is so very far above a beautiful horse, bird, or fish, that one should suppose the man who gave advice in a little book on the "Secrets of Generating" such angelic creatures should not have been convicted and sentenced to prison for a year, and made pay a fine of five hundred dollars, for an "Obscene Libel." The Libel should be thrown on the heads of those who depreciate and deteriorate this race of angels.

A CHILD that is born and bred in *true* relations to life and is raised in a physically and mentally healthful manner, will never have "*wicked and lewd passions*," still, will love God, Nature and Man ; and will like to gratify the *natural* desires, as the Creator ordained should be the case. But, a child that is born and bred in *false* relations to life, and is raised on gross and seasoned food, stimulating and narcotic beverages, foul air, indolent and constrained habits, will have his body and mind full of "*wicked and lewd passions*" and thoughts! "Unto the pure all things are pure," and *vice versâ*. Chew on this, ye lewd-thinking *vipers*.

THE Apostle Paul was an old dyspeptic, whose coatings of his stomach were well tanned (by high living) into sole-leather tissues, hence water could not be warmed-up and absorbed by his leather stomach; therefore, judging Timothy's organism to be in the same petrified condition, he said to Timothy : " Drink no longer water, but use a little wine for thy stomach's sake." If St. Paul had not been a fast Roman, revelling in highly seasoned food and wines in his early life, and would have done as Christ commanded, not having "judged" Timothy's stomach by his own, he might have handed down to us a purer and more perpetual piety. _____

I NEVER shall forget the pomposity of the old Judge, when he lectured me, before pronouncing his famous sentence upon me. He did it with such a *gusto ;*—but he little dreamt of the pity I had for the poor old man's memory, in his effort to disgrace an innocent man, which future generations will stigmatize as the boldest and most unjust ruling of any tyrant that ever disgraced public office. The following are his words:—

"The offence of which you have been convicted is one, which, to my mind, is of a grievous character. I know nothing which of itself tends more to the demoralization of society, and to the corruption of pure minds, and especially of the young, than a publication of the character of which you have been convicted.

"It should be the desire of every one in a community like this, or whether the community be great or small, to hold the minds, not only of the mature, but of the young, pure and untainted, and anything which tends to break down the natural modesty and purity of the human mind is subversive of the highest interests of our being.

"I think that the law has affixed to the offence of which you have been convicted, a mild penalty. I know of cases, of civil cases, in which it would be my duty, if the law warranted it, in extending the term of imprisonment which is provided by the act of Assembly; therefore, though I believe it my duty to impose upon you the full sentence provided by the act of Assembly, still, I feel it is but reasonable in itself.

"SENTENCE.—*The sentence of the Court is, therefore, that you pay a fine of* FIVE HUN-DRED DOLLARS, *and undergo an imprison-ment in the Philadelphia County Prison* FOR THE TERM OF ONE YEAR.

"HON. WM. S. PEIRCE, Presiding.

"*Philadelphia*, January 22nd, 1870."

He was so sorry that he could not *extend the penalty;* he told my wife he would like to give me $5000 fine and five years imprisonment, which was in keeping with his ruling out of my lawful evidence, and misconstruing the law to the Jury. I saw he was sorry that he had not the power to pronounce the death penalty upon me. The infinite Creator is competent to give him justice, if he did not give it to me. It is astounding how prejudice will carry some men beyond their manhood!

4

As an Ex-Judge—O. G. Chase—of West
Virginia, wrote me after perusing my trial,
so I have always felt; he said : " Dr. Landis,
there is nothing either in your book, '*Secrets
of Generation*,' or *Trial* of which *you* need
ever be ashamed.   The Court and prosecuting Attorney have thoroughly disgraced
themselves."

THE audacity of some rich men is shown
in my landlord, of whom I have rented a
public hall for the last seven years, and
whom I have always paid the rent before it
was due, except since in prison I owed him
two months' rent, when he visited me and
said : "*I* have not persecuted you any, you
cannot say that."   " Well then," said I,
" will you please take *half* cash for your
rent, until I come out of prison, or wait
altogether until I come out, and save me
from sacrificing my printing office."   " No,
sir, I want to be paid up in *full*, or if you
give me good security I will wait a while,"
he responded.   A fool or miser could a-k
no more.

THERE are too many writers, preachers, and lecturers who tell their hearers and readers to *do right*, but don't show them HOW to do it. To tell an apprentice to do a piece of work right, without *showing* him *how* to do it, would undoubtedly be followed by botchery. But it is dangerous to give the " *how*,"—this *how to do right*, sent me to prison; because, I told them *how* to make beautiful, sound, and perfect babies, and the sensualists considered this " HOW " obscene; hence, my chastisement for interfering with customs. If I had left the " *how* " alone, I might have had all sorts of engravings and wordings in my book; but the whole motive and object of poor me, *was* to show ignorant people, not holy experts, the " *how*; " to show them *how* to prevent diseases, unhappiness, and make them as happy as God designed, besides generating a perfect offspring! This matter is the very chief corner-stone, or fundamental principle of my piety, and I have the great law of nature, the Creator, and Jesus Christ to back me up in my scientific deductions.

THERE are people in this world who think they have a perfect right to their *own* opinions; have a perfect right to make (by any means) as much money (and retain it) as they please; that heaven and earth, and even the air belongs to them (hence they can perfume it with tobacco or anything else); that they have a sole right to liberty, and the concomitant matters and things that are found on His footstool, or in the realms of bliss above; all belong to their elect personages! It would be *nice*, if they would also claim the devil; for verily, methinks, he *will go* for a greater portion of their *little* souls; if they have not carried off everything, which would incapacitate him to heat up his gridirons!

WHAT is more charming than to see sweet, pure, innocent young people make love to each other, such as Miss Jones and myself did on papa Jones' old porch on moonlit nights? Was it not delicious? Yes—and we never thought of " *wicked and lewd pas-*

sions," such as were quoted, or spoken orig-
inally by Judge P——. "The law pro-
hibits the publication or sale of anything
which tends to excite in *us* wicked and lewd
passions." He acknowledged to possess such
wantonness, but we had none of it, had we,
Miss Jones? No, sir. I suppose it is owing to our plain living, and simple, natural
lives in this God-created country; but man
makes the cities; and the habits of these
fashionable Christians, like Judge P——,
naturally make them artificial and lewd!
Yes, that must be it. Oh, what a pity for such
misled people! You are right.

I HEAR people lamenting and dreading
old age. Oh, if they *only* were young again.
To me this is a puzzle, I *long* for old age;
for the sere and yellow leaf; for the gentle
passage toward the close of a *ripe* old age,
mellowing and dying, blessing and blessed;
and passing from earthly to heavenly spheres,
where the angel hosts, and friends and kindred all, who did *not* dread old age, will

4*

meet to part no more. It is the most glori-
ous thought of my life; and when I reflect
on my severe labors, trials, and persecutions,
I rejoice that sooner or later I shall retire
from this tumultuous world, and go to rest
amidst the bosoms of the blessed, where Father, Son, and Whole or Holy Spirit ever
adorn the countenances of the faithful. For
I dearly love beautiful countenances.

THE best and noblest quality that the
mind can possess is sincerity; the next to
this is willingness to learn and obey the
truth.

GOOD and great minds will not strike a
man when he is down, when he is confined
in a felon's cell, or after the battle is won.
Magnanimity enters freely into the composi-
tion of good metal, which will attract im-
maculate and lofty conception.

"*I*" KNOW nothing outside of myself; therefore, those who know nothing inside or out-

side of themselves, must not blame me for using *"I."*

KINDNESS and flattery may excel in gaining the goodwill of men and women, but they do not claim to be attributes of heaven when sprung into existence at the sacrifice of truth.

IF you will shut your mouth and open your eyes and ears, you may soon learn to rise above prejudice; *especially*, if you associate with wise people. Thusly, a " still tongue makes a wise head."

THAT Physiology which is not able to distinguish nourishment from stimulant; or, theory from actual knowledge; or, natural feeling from wantonness, is a false one, however popular it may be with uneducated naturalists or sham Christians. A TRUE Physiology shows *that state of man*, in which exists a *perfectly sound mind*, which is only found in a fully developed and sound body

TOXIC and Alterative Medicated Bitters
operate upon the living skins, tissues, or
mucous surfaces as the tanner's bark operates
upon the hides of animals,—they make leather
out of them, hence no more feeling in them,
nor growling by the human nerves. This
kind of logic is a better tonic and alterative,
if you comprehend it, and shun these petrifying stuffs, (trusting to God and Nature
when ill, with the injunction to *fast and
pray*,) than all the Bitters and Medicinal
Panaceas in christendom! The doctors and
newspaper men will be indignant over this
proclamation, because their advertised drug-
business will go defunct.

HEALTHY fruits contain a natural, or
godly, or God-created, proportion of water,
nutrition and innutrition needed by the
human system to keep the blood, nerves,
bones, flesh, and alimentary canal in a truly
normal state. There is no other one food
that does so contain all the component parts
of an unfallen Adam. Before the fall of

man, these fruits grew naturally in the Garden of Eden, and they were permitted to *freely,* not dyspeptically, *eat* of them. These fruits may be divided into mealy, acid, and oily fruits. The mealy make nerve and flesh ; the oily, bone, hair, nail, etc. ; and the acid cut or dissolve the food and aid in separating or secreting the various juices of the organism. Each contains a greater proportion of water. Allopathy and Sectarianism wide awake.

I HAVE taught, urged, and almost coerced upon the people sound physiological doctrines for many years, and have received nothing but scorn, contempt, ill-will, and persecution for my innovations, that I am getting disgusted with their ingratitude, but not with God's fixed laws of life; and when I get again upon *terra firma,* shall be less zealous than I was in former days. If their systems can stand all sorts of ignorant abuses, I can shut my eyes and grit my teeth at their suicidal barbarity ; but, to be compelled to see dear, innocent children suffer from these sins is *more* than I ever could endure and hold my mouth shut.

THE majority of persons are too ignorant to tell the difference between a scientific, wise man and a blustering quack.   This is another lamentable condition of this civilized community.

TWO-THIRDS of this people claim to be rather wise, when they do not even understand what makes muscles, nerves, or bones. They know more of wagons, houses, gold, and of fighting one another.

HE is a shallow-pated philosopher who denounces Christianity and the Bible, but withal quotes the latter to justify his acts, and to comfort others.   I am acquainted with many such.

HE who wishes *bonâ fide* happiness, and long joyous life, should try and keep his system remodelled by pure air, healthy food, fresh water, and an open conscience; instead of preserving or pickling it as if he were a dead herring.

WHEN a woman is once *really* in love, she is the best sticking plaster that was ever done up.

AMIABILITY seems to consist, in modern days, in white-lies, smooth tongues, and flattery. This is the trinity of fashionable piety, if " seeing is believing."

ONE day, when my two daughters were three and five years old, they sat at the heater in a cold room, when the oldest was explaining what she learned in Sabbath school about heaven,—she said to the younger one : " Heaven is a nice cool place, and hell is a hot burning place." " What," responded the baby talker, " did you say heaven was a cool place?" " Yes," replied her sister.

"Then," said she, shivering, "I'd rather go to hell where it's hot, wouldn't you, Emily?"

A LADY member of my church writes me: "If men are to be treated as you have been, for doing good, what inducement have others to become benefactors; you have suffered immensely from persecution for years, but this imprisonment excels all?" My dear sister, the only inducement others will have "for doing good" and becoming benefactors, will be an assurance from Christ and the Fountain Head of all wisdom and blessedness, that we have "fought the good fight," and when death sweeps us from amongst our persecutors we shall sit amidst the throng of the Saints!

IT seems quite a condescension for even dissipated, rude, ignorant persons to notice a convict, who is closely confined in a felon's cell; for, *of course*, the concluding idea strikes every one, who gazes at a prisoner, that he *is a criminal*, or a Judge and twelve

honest (?) Jurymen would not have sent him
there! As for prejudice, in this age, convicting a man who is innocent is beyond
belief; so then, grin and bear, until your
time expires, unless the Executive should be
honest enough to rise above party and
prejudice and set you free. This is all true,
but curiously insignificant so long as *you* are
not the victim. Wait awhile, may be your
turn comes next, for you are not safe under
such tyranny, no matter how pure and
innocent!

WHAT do the people think a person is
after; or what can be the motives of him,
who opposes vehemently the useless, abusive,
false customs of their choice? He cannot be
after their influence, nor their money, nor
their goodwill; because, to attain such would
require an opposite course of action. There
is only one answer to this question, and that
is, *that he has risen above self and bigotry,*
and seeing the perilous condition of society, he
labors to save them from pain, desolation and

5

damnation,—he is imitating the example of Jesus, to *heal the sick* and teach them how to obtain a natural, blissful career here, and a sure election to the hallowed realms of eternal life! In Scripture parlance, he is endeavoring to teach mankind to "*first seek the kingdom of God,*" when all else that is *necessary* will be added thereunto, whether it be lucre, raiment, food, or other concomitant of a godly life. God understands and loves him, because he keeps an eye single or pure to the normal welfare of His children; thereby glorifies God!

THE professed Christian who is afraid to die, for fear of going to hell, does not understand God, neither does he love and live-out Jehovah's fixed laws, or this nonsense and dread of going into the spheres above would be exchanged for love to go hence!

A RELIGIOUS PAPER says: "One of our correspondents proposes to furnish a few articles on Dr. Diehl's comments on Christ's

Descent into Hell." Would it not be wiser and better if these saints would learn to comprehend Christ's practical sermons on the mountain, and keep their mouths, stomachs, teeth, bones, flesh, nerves, brains, and blood clean, and trust the rest to God? Otherwise we fear when *they* "descend into hell," they will be so filthy, slippery, and heavy that they cannot rise again, but must remain and roast!

IT is better for a man to cultivate a taste for beautiful feminine arms, busts, legs, and faces, than for rum, tobacco, gross feeding, laziness and indifference to his salvation.

As much as I am opposed to fighting, I am fully convinced that *"Prize Fighters"* have given us better lessons for physical development, than gormandizing and sad-countenanced ministers, who suffer from preachers' sore throats, dyspepsia and consumption. I advise the latter to use a little more fistication.

For a man to get ahead of the age in which he lives, is as dangerous as to get his hand into another man's pocket; with this *special* caution, that in proportion as he makes a large success in drawing a prize, will he be less criminal than the presumptuous innovating renegade.

Whilst half dressed people, and especially ladies, will not benefit lewd Judges and sensualists, they will nevertheless do a mountain of good to pure and innocent people, because the more common a thing becomes the less attention and curiosity does it excite. Moreover, half the beauty of the angelic human form is buried from the sight of human eyes, and I cannot conceive how our mock-modest and lewd people will be able to go either to heaven or hell without having the thing indicted as an obscene nakedness!

A public official has no business to allow his prejudices to govern him in his official acts. A precocious man, by name of Gibbons, was the acting Prosecuting Attorney at the time of my mock trial, and the way he spread himself in exaggerating things against me, and insisted upon ruling out lawful evidence, was a caution; my counsel, in his able argument in answer to this bombast and unlawful bluster, said : "The District Attorney was incorrigible. He kept out the truth in Winnemore's case, and our client was convicted and executed. I told Wm. B. Mann, District Attorney at that time, that the sceptre of his power would be taken and placed in other hands. I hope the *present* District Attorney (Gibbons) will profit by his example."

Truly my counsel's warning or prophecy has been fulfilled. This third day of May, 1870, I read in the papers that *Gibbons* has been removed from the office; it literally belonging to *Furman Sheppard*, Esq. Mr. Gibbons did struggle *hard* to hold the office to which he was *not* entitled, neither was he fit for it. God works in a mysterious manner,

5*

Charley Gibbons. When you seek office again, we hope to be about to do our duty in getting sound-minded and honorable men to fill public offices. Where are the $20,000 ?

MODERN Spiritualism and Orthodox Sectarianism seem to me, if "seeing is believing," to be riding the same hobby to death—Spiritualists depend altogether upon the Spirits—the etherealized—the gauzy—for salvation or happiness, whilst living in real, material, earthly life ; and the Sectarians rely upon "Faith" without learning and living out the laws of the growth and natural development of human nerves, bones and flesh, whilst travelling over this earth, which is the preparatory stage upon which the soul or spirit depends for its perfection, its fulness of power and grace divine through the medium of the body. Why don't they attend to this, their *right* business, of causing physical perfection *first*, when they would surely receive the full fruition of their godly lives ; whereas, they grabble and dabble with things *beyond*, before they are prepared for the very thing that they blow and howl about so much? It puts me in mind of a lot of silly school boys, who would fight about things which they could not understand— for example, one boy saith to the others: " I know a place where apples grow without the apple tree." The others respond : " You fool, there must be a *tree*, and a healthy one too, before good apples can grow upon it;" finally, they all agree that there must be a tree *first*, but it matters not where or how it grows; that it is not necessary to give it any attention, all that is requisite is to believe in eating the fruit. But we ask—does not the fruit often become defective, wormy, or the tree grow barren, when the natural soil and elements are withheld from its roots, body and branches? Have ye eyes and ears, and cannot ye behold your own boogaboo?

NONE so blind as those who choose to be, and none so deaf as those who hear with both ears *open* or both *shut*, either letting

nothing in or letting *in* and *out* simulta-
neously. Therefore nothing sticks.

THE New Testament speaks of three
Baptisms, the Water, Holy Spirit, and Fire
or Hell Baptisms, each meaning plunged in
over head and ears, and teetotally covered
up. The Fire or Hell one gets more by
double than its share; "if the court know
herself, and we think she do." Water
washes away the physical dirt, opens the
eight millions of pores, and makes room for
the Whole or Holy Spirit to enter, if other
things are equal ; but, when this is not the
case the Fire in Hell fries out the dirt and
crisps the body so that the Whole or Holy
Spirit could not get in, if it would ! But,
you need not be, any ways, alarmed or
troubled about the latter, for it does *not*
want to go where penitence and sound sense
do not prevail. The Devil attends to such !

THE war has ended, and I have mustered
out the *"Sharp-Shooter,"* because the vic-

tory is won, and I am acknowledged KING amongst Christians; because, I have had a *mock* Trial, and have been, and am now, imprisoned for shooting the hallowed truth through old fogy brains until they gave me the prize! So were the Prophets persecuted before us! This is more truthful than poetic.

THE Shakers evidently are the purest and best Christians on the globe; having "all things common;" self and filth of mind or body do not enter into their piety. A pure, good, honest people!

WHEN I get out of prison I must do either one of the following things:—First, walk straight through the Pharisees and giddy, impenitent worldlings; or, secondly, repent and turn hypocrite and fashionable thief, tyrant and usurper, for I cannot do anything half. It is my imperative nature to go the whole figure or die. It would be much *nicer* to be hewn out differently, but

as I did not make myself, I have no choice
in the matter.

COURTING is fine fun, think some people,
but sour grapes with those who turn it into
sensuality and frivolity.   Let it only be
done with clear-headed and prayerful con-
sideration, or you will rue it when it is too
late.

THERE are some people so blasted ignorant that they cannot see how a man can do
any good except with money.   It is money
that does far more *ill* than good in this
world.   They look at it as the best friend,
because they find that with it anything almost that they want, whilst journeying here,
can be bought; God's laws and inspiring
power cannot be reached with *filthy lucre*,
and therein lies all good.

WHEN persons get too bold in villany
they often find a sudden down-come, even
from great wealth to extreme poverty.   In

time of health and wealth prepare for sick-
ness and poverty by storing up in your
heads a sound understanding of the "laws
of growth;" "laws of cure," and "laws of
nature," on the one hand; and on the other,
by establishing a true Christian Treasury,
where things are held in common by the
members of the Church!

HE alone is respectable who respects himself and his Creator; and who by so doing,
masters his propensities and learns to mind
his own business, whilst he does not fail to
do his duty to his fellows. He is not
jealous, selfish, penurious, avaricious nor
malicious; but is a light to the world, and
a "paragon of animals;" and the opposite
sex soon learns to respect and love that one,
little short of idolatry, no matter if he *never*
wore a suit of broadcloth; or if he happens
to be a she, if she never wore horse-hair
busts, hoops, flounces, silks, satins or Grecian
Benders, but has simply exhibited a plump
flesh and blood development, without rouge,
powder, or muskrat stinks!

In time of prosperity you have hosts of friends; then you do not need them; but in the hour of adversity they "skedaddle" like sheep when a wolf is after them. If the human race could only be made to understand and appreciate that as long as a true Progressive Christianity is overlooked, and there is no union of action in this direction, so long it is an unsafe world to bring and raise children in. Why will ye be living in jeopardy; risking your happiness here and hereafter? Oh! Repent, dear reader, and become an earnest follower of Christ and the Truth!

Do you seek health, or beauty, or happiness? If you do, remember that pure, fresh, outside *air* day and night, and *especially* when sleeping, is the foremost agency in God's vocabulary for the retaining and regaining of these graces. Angels inhabit *pure* air, and Imps *foul* air. Like begets like, without dislike.

To live long, to keep healthy and vivacious, abstain from eating grease (except oily fruits), spices, preserved dishes and concentrated varieties; also shun artificial beverages, drinking pure fresh *hot* water, at meals, if dyspeptically inclined; and as for tobacco and other drugs, throw them to the "dogs" and "swine," but even they, if four legged ones, will not condescend to touch them. "Are ye not much better than they? O, ye of *little* faith," with all your pious blowing about being saved *by* "Faith." Your plum pudding smells strong and is not eatable, hence the disregard and distaste for Christianity. "Woe unto you Scribes, and Pharisees, Hypocrites, for ye devour widows' houses, and for a pretence make long prayers; therefore ye shall receive the greater damnation;" and ye proselyte the innocent and drag them into filthy and poisonous habits, fitting them for hell and the devil!

Do you wish to follow the dictates of my

6

persecutors? If so, I will give you the first lesson to the dignity of the crowd, which travels on the "broad road."

1.—Marry for lust, money, position or spite, but *not for Love*. Reserve your "*wicked and lewd passions*."

2.—Hate homely, puny, sickly children, but make them, from the first jump in matrimony, by the wagon load, and blame it on God.

3.—Have family worship regularly and let your neighbors know it, then "go it" into anything and everything that tastes. feels, smells or looks good, with this caution, that you have "Faith" in blaming natural results that follow ignorance and fashionable slopping unto God.

4.—Feed the babies on anything that is palatable and handy, asking no questions for conscience' sake; and when they get sick, give them drops or pills of some kind, no matter which they be, and by the time they are six or ten years old they are fine specimens of stomach dyspeptics, which opens the door to the apothecarys' and doctors' pockets; besides, being mentally dyspeptics at twelve or fifteen, which opens the door to the parsons and God-dictators, and having now started in respectable, modest, fashionable, civilized business-life, all you need do is, to trust to, and blame on God the results, and follow your own *feelings*, no matter if your "*nerves of feeling*" are half drunk, half dead, half fool, half pickled, half befuddled, or entirely defunct, as long as a spark of life remains, *stir it up* with a fiery hot medicated poker (Cayenne Pepper, Corrosive Sublimate, Potash, or sich), but remember, that you blame it *all*, EVERY BIT OF IT, on God!

CHRIST, the truth, or nature, or life, or the inner man heals every wound and ill that flesh is heir to, provided usable, compatible, natural agencies (not poisons) and influences are used to make conditions favorable for the living or Christ-powers to work upon. Likewise did Jesus and his Apostles, as we do, heal the sick without drugs. What sectarian church follows the example of their Master? Modern Spiritualists claim to heal by "laying on hands," but that is a small part of the work, so long as they do not teach and restrict their patients and sinners to live upon the pure "fruits of the earth for meat." "Laying on of hands" may energize the nerves and do some good, but to say that it rebuilds or remodels the bodily structures, and making them solid and sound, without recourse to natural food and drink, is as great a farce as *Sectarian Faith-Talk*. You might as well go to the weaver, who fills up the warp with silken woof, and get the Spiritualist to lay his hands on the silken woof, or food, or filling, and say, Presto, change into cotton, as to say, Swallow pork, grease, spices, tobacco, etc., and heal, which means rebuild, or grow sound bodily tissues. Have ye eyes; then see and act like men, not fools? A combination of right things will do the work alone!

EVERY day takes a link out of our earthly chain, and instead of your chain growing longer, when you transgress natural laws, Christian or truthful laws, it gets shorter *twofold;* that is, by violation of law you shorten your days here, and make yourself less talented, and in the life to come you will have to hunt for centuries in pain and misery until you find the lost links, before you can be baptized with the Whole or Holy Spirit.

PLEASE, good reader, imagine YOURSELF confined in a felon's cell for one year and compelled to pay five hundred dollars fine, and all to gratify the wrath of a prejudiced people, who did not like you to be an honest benefactor, as I have proved in Court I was, and shall prove to be over and over again, if God grants me life, until I get out of this place. My poor children and wife need my services for support.

THE self-styled *moral* " Philadelphia Pub-

lic Ledger " gloried that I would have hours
for "*reflection and meditation*" during my
incarceration, but lamented that I was not
sent to the Penitentiary; and *now* I will
take him at his "glory," and " reflect and
meditate " honestly over the acts of the Pro-
prietor of this oracle, hoping that he will
pardon me if I shall be compelled to tread
upon his toes.

If he is a moral man he would scarcely
grow so fat in wealth by the earnings of the
poor, charging (those who can scarcely rake
and scrape enough money together to keep a
shanty over their heads and buy a crust of
bread) *twenty to twenty-five cents a line for
an advertisement,* which he should give to
them for five cents a line. No wonder he
swims in *filthy lucre,* and builds himself a
castle costing one hundred thousand dollars ;
and splurges and shows off now and then in
a left-handed donation of a few thousand
dollars to "get glory of men," etc. How
does my "reflection and meditation " suit
the man who would not advertise my lawful

business, but could editorially spread false-
hoods about me after I was in Prison? This
is morality and piety at a vengeance! God
forgive him, or Hell may burn him, *lucre*,
castle, and all to cinders.

If this "Public Ledger" man had been
as magnanimous as wealthy, he would not
have struck a poor, struggling, honest Reformer, nor falsely accused him of being a
"*child murderer*," after he was down, in
Prison, and could not defend himself; trying
thereby to disgrace and injure this innocent
man and wife, and their defenceless children! But his peculiar *morality* allows anything that money can buy or cover up.
Such are my "reflections and meditations;"
whether there is any logic in my deductions, I am willing the reader shall decide
for himself, with this observance—that I
pity such soft-headed moral fools!

CHARITY begins at home, but where is
home, sweet, sweet home? In heaven, or
in *true* happiness. Then our charities must

go all over the land, amongst the nations,
because a few cannot make true happiness
on this earth, but many combined in well-
doing can. This seems a paradox, and in
opposition to the few who shall only find
the narrow path that leads to heaven. Yes,
yes, but you must remember when the
wicked, hollow, shrivelled spirit leaves this
mortal coil it is sent to spheres that are
separated from happy realms, hence they
can no more chew tobacco and spit the filth
unto good people, nor puff the vile fumes
of the hellish weed into purified faces;
neither can they contaminate the heavenly
atmosphere with fashionable perfumes and
stinks which would render foul and unhappy
the purest saintly attributes. It is charity
to all mankind to expose the truth, however
hard it may hit sinners! Hypocrisy and
flattery are not charity, but cruelty; neither
is blackmailing to save a scoundrel from
chastisement a charity, but an injury, because it only emboldens him.

WHAT shall a man do when he is to write or speak and is out of ideas, and empty of thought? Well, do as the writer now does; write it down, and continue on writing down his empty-brain condition, and by the time he has exposed it all, may be some new thought or idea will present itself. But, suppose such is not the case, what then? I hardly know how to answer this last question, excepting to be uncivil and tell him *he is a liar!*—What! you call me a liar?—Yes, sir.—How dare you be so rude?—Oh, my dear fellow, I am only telling the naked *truth*, and I have often heard you say that the truth was never rude, but should always be told; and have you not been writing thoughts and ideas all this time that you were grumbling you had none? Now, what is all this but a lie? Sure enough, I have an idea and a thought— and that is, that it is just as civil to call a man a liar, when he is one, as to call him a saint when he is none. The next time you have no ideas or thoughts, just clap your mind upon hypocrites, and you will not fail to find mountains of them! Yaw wole.

Good nonsense is often better sense than what is accepted as *common sense*. The latter is seldom *sound sense* as the world goes. It is but common sense, if I love a beautiful damsel, that I should be allowed to embrace her, but *sound sense* says, nay. It is common, however, for men to attempt just such sense, and they often succeed where *sound sense* cries against the act; especially if the fellow has a good wife and children at home, whom he neglects.

I am in favor of "Woman's Rights," since I saw so many pimps in Court during my trial. These demons were on the alert for every word that had any reference to the chaste and loving sex, and the moment they would catch a word that could have any bearing upon the *holiest* functions, and most vital organs of Mothers, they snickered, grinned and laughed. The Judge himself endeavored to get off several jokes at the expense of women, and the District Attorney found my book too "filthy and obscene to go upon the records of the honorable Court," as if sexual organs, and child bearing, and womb complaints, etc., etc., were proper matters to record in Court. The "Obscenity" of the thing was to bring such matters into a Court that is composed of "wicked and lewd passioned" men, who forget that their own mothers were women; hence, I deem it imperative to have such masculine cattle driven from Court Rooms and place women there, who I am convinced would appreciate and comprehend God's mechanism, and the concomitant matters of maternity, far better, and would not badger female witnesses as did that District Attorney and his associates. Woman must be the "coming man," or we are gone up spout.

HE who interprets the Bible in such a manner as to make it conflict with the great fixed Law of Nature is a false expounder of

Gospel truths, and there is to this day only one living man who explains the Scriptures scientifically. It is I, presumptuously.

WHY, and at whose pleasure, I was arrested. One of the officers who arrested me in my pulpit has visited me several times since in prison, and he told me that if I had remained in my own Hall, in the northern part of the city, and had not advertised to go to the large central Concordia Hall, I would not have been arrested. Said he: "Mayor Fox got a few letters asking him to arrest Dr. Landis, who had published several obscene books, and by announcement in the papers will preach next Sunday evening, on obscene things, in Concordia Hall; this man is continually violating the law and should be arrested. The Mayor, not knowing any better, ordered Mr. Brenieser to go to your office and buy a book; he did so; and on Saturday the warrant was sworn out, and ordered by the Mayor to be held until Sunday evening, until you would appear

at Concordia Hall to preach, where we
arrested you, and you know the result. But,
I could never have believed that it would
result in your imprisonment like this, and I
believe the Mayor is sorry he ever arrested
you."

Yes, well he may be sorry ; or if he is not,
he carries a tough face. But I forgive him
for this outrage and persecution ; because,
God often uses weak tools to bring His
disciples, and expounders of truth, before the
people, and persecution does this better than
anything else, for so persecuted they the
prophets and good men, who still live in the
memory of the people with a *kindly* feeling.

It has always been a Religious principle
with me not to look on the dark side of the
picture ; not to believe that people mean as
badly as their evil acts show. And I always
endeavor to find, *in my own mind*, an excuse
for sinful and criminal conduct ; therefore,
when I was told, by friends, after my arrest,
and previous to my Trial, as also since in

7

prison, that I was "*convicted before I was tried*," I did not, *could not*, believe that our officials were so debased as to trample justice under foot. But, alas! I was disappointed, and I am now satisfied that it makes little difference whether a person violates the law or not, if the *Pharisees* get a spite at a man or woman, he or she goes to limbo. This is a "*Republic*," at *two-forty* on the plank road to hell!

They were not satisfied with only imprisoning me, but I was not three weeks lodged in my cell until they smuggled poisoned figs to me; but as I was foully arrested and maliciously convicted, I desired to smell my way along, hence examined these figs by opening them, and there detected, in profusion, Arsenic, nicely piled inside of about one half of them. No sooner had I announced this attempt to poison me than I was very roughly handled, seeming to me as though some one was highly indignant at my continued existence. It is a pity that they could not send me hence, for I would rather go than stay amongst such sinners.

THE Earth, or Soil, is stimulated, heated and forced as much as Man ; hence so much mildew, vermin and rotten trash in market.

"SLAVE to no sect, but look through nature up to nature's God,"—my piety to a dot, and the only *genuine* article in existence.

WHENEVER a man is rich enough, or able in any manner, to run a *large* establishment, he is respectable and his acts are not criminal, if ever so foul.   As examples :— To keep a bawdy house as large as the Continental or St. Nicholas Hotel is decent ; but, if it were some starving widow keeping a boarding house for a few persons, whose actions and business she would not dare to question, if ever so questionable, for fear of losing her little, mean income, her gossiping neighbors and city detectives would soon report her as a criminal.

Again, a man may keep a little shanty where persons play games for pennies and he will be arrested, whilst a Bank President or wealthy Broker can gamble and cheat the innocent out of tens of thousands and be a "bull" or a "bear," who is lionized as a generous, philanthropic millionaire.

Still, again, a man may devote his *all* to alleviating the sufferings of the distressed; whilst a mean, miserly minded "swine" may grab and reserve all he can get honestly and dishonestly for himself, and when these two oppositely disposed persons are brought before the world, or before a Tribunal of Justice, the rich miser will be lauded for his *manliness*, whilst the philanthropist is esteemed a criminal and "obscene" wretch. So *you* pharisees go; but, God and good sound minded men detest the injustice and stupid prejudice and rascality of such conduct!

THERE are a hundred tears shed in the Theatres, whilst one is squeezed out in Sectarian Churches; unless it be the gall-tears, caused by being indignant at Theatre-goers. A good Theatre is better than a bigoted Church any day.

I HAVE had nothing but opposition since I have been a baby. I have had to fight against kindred and strangers in my zeal to bring about the greatest Reformation that man ever was engaged in; but "these things moved me not," for I was intuitively urged to go on in what I knew was right, if all the world disowned and despised me! I have done so, and I have nothing at all to regret, whilst I was true to my inner man. I have been rich and poor in worldly wealth, but I always felt more contented and happy when I did not own a penny, but was able to earn daily bread for myself and family. This imprisonment however takes me away from my business; hence my beloved family must suffer for the necessaries until I shall be free again to serve them. It is no trouble to make *lucre*.

WHEN haughty and cowardly pharisees once get their over-awing-power on you, they are, like all tyrants and usurpers, cruel and brave; but the moment they find an

7*

overwhelming open enemy, they slink away like whipped curs, and dissemble and whimper like innocent lambs. No wonder Jesus despised their ways: we ditto!

JUDGE CHASE writes me : " Dr. Landis,— Shame will visit the Judge in his grave, who occupied the bench during your trial. He acted as Court, Prosecuting Attorney and Jury. I would rather be a Dr. Landis, than a Judge ——. Pray for his conversion, and forgive the man who disgraced himself and his office." I freely forgive him, and I hope God will have mercy on him, as he needs it.

WHEN a scoundrel in office commits a crime, violates the law in his official capacity, and inflicts the penalty upon his fellows, which by right belongs on his shoulders, he chuckles and glories in his villany, and assumes a virtue that insults every angel in heaven and good man on earth; whereas the imps join him in his delight.

It actually seems to be the delight of this people to make one-another unhappy, instead of loving one-another!

The piety which fears that open discussion will draw its followers away from it, is rotten to the core. Piety, to be sound, must rest in the bosom of truth, and the more you agitate and stir it, the more brilliant it becomes, because it is a precious jewel; but, if, that piety is simply a cloak, or make-believe, and you stir it, it will be like unto filth, the more agitated the more it will stink. Vulgar but lofty truths.

It is a very incomprehensible matter to me, how our most refined, fastidious and sanctimonious professors of Christianity can object to the use of plain, vulgar or common language. Jesus used no other, and he did not hesitate in calling a liar—a liar. And he often used such words as stink, fool, viper, hell, damnation, hypocrites, pharisees, circumcision, womb, whore, dog, swine, eunuch, fornication, open act of the same, etc. ; but, when *I* used such words to illustrate scientific physiological law, they arrested and convicted me for an " Obscene Libel." Do not these acts of my enemies crucify the Christ—the truth—by such persecution, and stamp me a *true* follower of Jesus ? Certainly.

I AM not opposed to Theatres, but if *I* am guilty of " Obscenity," then are all our actors and theatre-goers guilty of the same offence ; and they are the *most* guilty, because, they indulge in sensual sights and for mere gratification purposes, whilst my motive and acts were to cause people to enjoy life *naturally*, and thereby benefit the race, without any wantonness or lust about it. Consistency, thou art a jewel, but art in modern days wofully abused. Do these remarks fit any of my persecutors ? If so, I hope they will have more charity for me, and give honor and justice where it is due.

ANY ignorant person thinks he has as good a right to give his opinion on topics of health, morality and piety as a strictly scientific mind, who has devoted a long and entire lifetime to studying the same. Therefore, it is really no credit for any one to sacrifice himself for the good of humanity, because, the untutored ignoramus is as soon believed as the sage and philosopher; the people *themselves* do not take sufficient interest in these matters of body, soul and spirit to become competent judges who is wise or unwise; hence, an innocent Reformer may be mistaken for a criminal.

TRUTH would be popular and acceptable in any guise, if it would fill the pocket with gold and elect the inksuckers and pharisees into Moses' seat. But, as the contrary is the case, the expounders may look out for squalls, if they get too bold in its promulgation.

YOU will believe me, almost to a man, if I truthfully assert that I came very near poisoning my prison-keeper and two "runners." This would have been an awful crime, I admit. Don't you think so? And you believe me guilty in my mind to commit this act; but, when I tell how it would have occurred, if I had not been detecting the matter, you will *not* believe me. This is the way:—Poisoned figs having been smuggled into my cell, for *myself* to swallow and die on; but, as I had often handed my keeper and two prison-runners some of my edibles, I was about dealing out to them these poisoned figs—and had already knocked at the cell door for them to come and get them, when they did not come immediately; in the meantime I opened the package and thought I would eat a few, but opened them and thus discovered the poison. Hence burned them.

THERE is a certain stage of some men's lives, when they should be brave enough to become egotistical. It is at that period when they have become masters of their business. But, before they have reached the *acme* of perfection in their vocations, they should be modest, willing to learn even from a fool or enemy; *in fact*, the latter is the only way, in modern days, that any one can become master of his business. Jesus never gave an opinion, because he was truth personified, and he always said, *I am the way, and the life, and the truth,* etc. Truth is always egotistical, and so are truly good and great men; the soft blabber of the ignorant worldling and pharisee to the contrary notwithstanding. There are too many erroneous opinions polished up by charlatan Editors, Authors and Preachers, that ought to be torn to flinders, when a healthier intelligence would rule the land. Piety does not consist of opinions.

It is a pity that the Sabbatarian Pharisees cannot induce God to stop the grass from growing on their holy Sabbath Day. And above all, for God to let such immense hail fall as this Sabbath Day fell, is shameful; that is, if Sabbatarianism is correct.

My persecution was sprung upon me with great force, when I began, about six years since, the agitation of the Sunday City Car Question. I preached, lectured and wrote in favor of our street cars running on Sundays, until I got them to run, and this was the first fire which I kindled in the sweet bosoms of the Sabbatarians; but, since the cars run, they all ride in them; however, they forget to thank me for forcing this Christian charity and convenience upon them. They are short-sighted and short-memoried. These are the lambs who conspired to arrest and imprison me.

———

CHRISTIANS should not become persecutors, nor tormentors; but, they ought to be the saviours of the fallen, and forgiving the penitent sinner, as God forgave them when they became Christians! Is this sound logic; does it chime with the teachings of Christ, Truth and sound sense, or is it vague and valueless? Saints of Sectarianism, will you be kind enough to answer me through your oracle, the "*Philadelphia Public Ledger?*" I am a poor convict, and wish to be converted to the *genuine* Gospel!

FEELINGS change with the change of bodily structures. A person who feeds on Eden Fruits will *think* and *feel* naturally, hence, godly. A person who feeds on a plain animal and vegetable diet, will think less and feel more than is strictly natural. And a person who feeds on a highly seasoned, concentrated, gaily barbecued, and chiefly animal diet, does *not think at all*, he only feels; and that feeling is unnatural, barbarous and swinish. The latter prefers plenty of money, to be able to buy plenty of sensual food, and neither scruples at, nor detests, plenty of women; and pays preachers, doctors and lawyers to do his thinking, but he is *sure* to do all his own feeling! And very sickly and lewd be it.

THE devil loves to be genteel, smooth-tongued, oily and sleek, because these are

8

the best baits that he can use in angling in this terrestrial pool of corruption and mock modesty. He finds that they bite so well with these baits that he sometimes gets tired out with handling the hosts of suckers that so greedily swallow the dainty bites.

My Prison-keeper thinks that my "scrape I got myself into, by getting into prison," will injure me so much that I wont be able to do any business, or draw any audiences, for years to come. We'll see about that, when I get out and about again. My idea is otherwise, but I may be mistaken; there is no telling.

My enemies were *really* so ignorant as to have supposed that a mock trial and malicious imprisonment would disgrace me so as to cause my ruination; but, I will handle them in such a manner for this outrage as to astonish their ignorance and impudence. With their equals this will hold good, but I consider it a vice to have their good will, and therefore care not for it.

A MAJORITY of a small minority is sufficient for one man to desire for a successful
reform; *in fact*, the majority of a small minority of good and wise people is equal, if
not superior, to the great majority of the
whole nation. Few popular men ever receive the plaudits of a greater number; *if
they do*, they are *de*formers, instead of *re*-
formers; because the devil has already secured by far the great majority.

IT will always be found by close obser-
vation that the roughest men have the best
and warmest hearts; because they can appreciate as well as depreciate; and embrace
good as well as deface ill; and drink-in as
well as throw-out! They are like good
fruit trees, having the roughest side outside,
whilst pure sap, milk and honey run
throughout every blood vessel, which deposit
an excrement that forms the bark, protect-
ing the inner life against the contaminations
of foreign things! Nature herself is rough
and smooth betimes.

Lot's daughters made their father drunk and had intercourse with him, to continue the seed of his loins; each of them had a baby by her father. If I should even print, much less advocate, or do such an act, I would be arrested by Mayor Fox, indicted by a low and lewd Grand Jury, and in less than a week be sentenced to one year imprisonment and five hundred dollars fine for an "Obscene Libel;" still, the old Bible, which relates the above story, is read in boarding schools, where Judge Peirce wanted "Secrets of Generation" to be proper to be read, or be esteemed "Obscene." Highflying consistent pressure, this is, or I am a fool.

I have just discovered that I have picked up involuntarily that delightful, lively, wide-awake malady, in vulgar parlance called the "*Itch.*" I can soon cure myself of it, if my boss will permit me to take a daily alcoholic sweating, but I guess he wants me to take drugs, prescribed by a little huge smoke-pipe doctor, who belongs to this celebrated hotel. Who is a butcher.

I AM promised to be let loose next Saturday, May 14th, 1870 ; but, whether or not such will be the case, depends altogether upon the honor and feelings of Governor Jno. W. Geary. I hope he'll never get out of his gear until he ungears me.

MY page, as well as my time, is drawing to a close, and as the last part of a speech should always be best, I hope some very bright "Prison Thoughts" may finish this stupid lot of expressions, which I have put down as they flitted through my brain. I never profess to possess any wit, but solid grit.

I ASKED Mr. Perkins, the Superintendent of this honorable prison, to allow me to give myself a few alcoholic vapor baths for the "*Itch*," which the filthy place inoculated me with, but he refuses to grant my request, and thinks (in fact, says) his doctors must treat me; he is determined to drug me, but I'll die first. One of his M. D.'s sucks the

8*

nastiest big pipe all the time around prison, which is more against the law than to grant me the privilege to treat myself. Mr. P. thinks he owns this shanty. I think he better have a successor very soon. His sectarian disposition should not domineer.

IT is as easy to find fault as kiss a tame lass; but sometimes very provoking to find the devil has been flirting with you.

HUMAN beings have "*souls*" (but they mean Spirits) "*to save*," is an old saying; however, brutes do •*not* have "souls to save;" still, the way farmers and breeders of brutes select the best blooded stock to breed young cattle and care for them, by feeding the brutes upon material that they *know* makes good blood, is lawful and chaste; whilst human beings, who have "souls to save," can be born and bred under the influences of lager beer, rum, tobacco, trash for food, foul air, indolence, mental and physical constraint, mock modesty,

hypocrisy, ignorance, fashion and folly; cap-
ping the sweet climax by convicting the
man, as an "Obscene Libellist," who incul-
cates equal care upon rational as irrational
creatures. Swine, *thou* art glorified, and
thy offspring continues in his swinishness;
but man, thou flappest also into swinishness, and thereby losest thy manhood, thy
beauty, thy godly attributes, and seest filth
in the fixed law of thine own Creator; because thine eyes are lagered, smoked, brined,
peppered, drugged, preserved, pickled and
dirty; hence, thy brain is befuddled and thy
intellect is barren, whilst thy morality and
piety lies in thy stomach and still lower
down. Thou art a sensualist, "wicked and
lewd passioned" lout. Good-bye, my best
wishes to thee, and my prayers for thy pardon; thou needest it badly.

DR. S. M. LANDIS'

Medical and Surgical Institute,

No. 13 North Eleventh St., above Market,

PHILADELPHIA, PA.

THE Physiological Expert is capable of treating *all kinds of diseases*, that flesh is heir to, with equal success ; at least, I have been so blessed in an extensive practice of twenty years. However, I have treated more sexual diseases by far than any other kind, owing probably to the fact, that I have continually lectured on private sexual matters for twenty years; but, I will wager any amount that my success will be equally great in consumption, or any other complaint. Let all sick people, of either sex, who have failed to be restored to health after they have exhausted everything else, consult me, and I will be honest and candid with them ; if I cannot do anything for them, I will say so, but if I decide a case curable, I warrant to eradicate the malady.

ADMINISTER NO INTERNAL DRUGS.

1. The Hygienic Agencies and Influences I rely upon for growing the bodily structures sound are : Animal Magnetism, Pure (Oxygenated) Air, Water, Sleep, Natural Food, Light, Rest, Exercise, Temperature, Clothing, and the regulation of the Passions.

2. The Medical Agencies of my own invention, and secured by Letters Patent, consist of my *Improved Turkish Bath;* Compound Electro-Magnetic Equalizer, and Compound Organic Syringing Apparatus.

3. The Surgical Appliances are the most improved extant.

MEDICAL CONSULTATION OFFICE HOURS,

By myself, every week-day, 7 to 11 A. M., and Monday and Thursday Evenings, 5 to 8 o'clock, at above place.

Improved Turkish Bath, only 50 cents each. For *males,* open 6 A. M., to 10 P. M., and Sundays 6 to 10 A. M. For *females,* separate bath and open by a lady superintendent from 7 A. M., to 5 P. M., only on week-days.

Assistant Physicians in Institute all the time. Medical Consultation by letter strictly confidential. Letters must have return stamp enclosed or no notice will be taken of them.

DR. LANDIS' BOOKS.

Secrets of Generation (that caused
   his imprisonment), sold sealed, . $1.00
Sense and Nonsense, on all topics
   concerning Human Affairs, . . 2.00
Health Cook Book, ... 1.00
Key to Love; The Science of Fasci-
   nation, ... 25
Key to Heaven, ... 10
*Private Lectures on Courtship
   and Marriage,* etc., ... 25
Prison-Life Thoughts. Paper, . 40
   Cloth 75
Sold by all News Dealers and Book Stores,
or will be sent pre-paid upon receipt of price
Address all orders and letters to

DR. S. M. LANDIS,

13 NORTH ELEVENTH STREET,

PHILADELPHIA.

———◦◦◦———

Dr. Landis' Lecture-Room and College
are in the same building, at 13 N. 11th St.,
Phila., where he lectures every Sunday at 7.30,
and Tuesday Evening at 8 o'clock, on Reformed,
Illustrated Physiological and Medical Subjects.

Students of both sexes educated by his *Short-Hand System*, as expert practising Physicians and Surgeons, also Rights of the Improved Turkish (Portable) Bath for sale, with or without the Electro-Magnetic Equalizer, and Compound Organic Syringing Apparatus.

N. B.—Private instruction given to married or marrying men and women to prevent the function of too rapidly increasing and multiplying. My means are infallible, natural and instead of being injurious, are beneficial to the health and beauty! *All* married people should be perfect masters over these matters, bogus enactments to the contrary notwithstanding.

THE END.

www.ingramcontent.com/pod-product-compliance
Lightning Source LLC
Chambersburg PA
CBHW031438270326
41930CB00007B/775